RC

GIL FAGIANI

Second Edition

Rain Mountain Press
New York City
2007

Price: $10.00

ISBN: 0-9786105-3-9

For reprint permission contact:
Rain Mountain Press
68 East Third Street, Suite 16
New York, NY 10003

LAYOUT AND DESIGN:
David G. Barnett
Fat Cat Graphics
Wekiva Springs Road, Suite 100
Longwood, FL 32779

PRINTED BY Publishers Graphics, Carol Stream, IL

Cover art by Jim Pignetti

First Printing: September, 2005
Second Printing: February, 2007, Revised and Expanded

Fagiani, Gil.
Rooks / by Gil Fagiani. -- 2nd ed.
p. cm.
ISBN 0-9786105-3-9 (pbk. : alk. paper)
1. Military cadets--Poetry. I. Title.
PS3606.A2655R66 2007
811'.6--dc22   2007017435

ROOKS

"A Rook is lower than the deepest bucket of whale shit in the deepest part of the ocean."

—Unofficial definition of a freshman cadet at Pennsylvania Military College

Cara Jennifer,

Auguri infiniti !

6/22/11

Gil

Rain Mountain Press
68 East Third Street, Suite 16
New York, NY 10003

CONTENTS

Part I

Part II

Art work by Jim Pignetti.

Officer's profile taken from the 1964 P.M.C. Yearbook.

Gil Fagiani's cadet photo taken from the 1967 P.M.C. Yearbook.

Former cadet obituaries taken from *The PMC Alumnus*, 1966-68.

Thanks to Dave Ellis, Class of 1965, for the corrected version of the unofficial definition of a freshman cadet.

Thanks to John Bullock at www.OldChesterPa.com for the Pennsylvania Military College photographs.

Special thanks to Jan Alexander for facilitating the author's access to Widener University's P.M.C. archives.

INTRODUCTION TO THE FIRST EDITION

The military legacy at Pennsylvania Military College went back 114 years when the cadet corps was phased out in 1972, and the school became Widener College. In January 2002, I began to work on a collection of poems inspired by my four years at P.M.C. (1963 to 1967). My motivation was two-fold: to rescue from obscurity a poignant and formative period of my life, and to explore the military ethos in the face of the dramatic militarization of American society following the attack on the World Trade Center. I decided to focus on my freshman – or "rook" – year, because it was when the assimilation process from civilian to military life was most intense, and the school's regulations, values, and traditions most emphasized. However, to better convey the spirit of the '60s in Chester, I have included other events and cultural phenomena, that strictly speaking, occurred after 1963-64. Having said that, I want to state clearly that "Rooks" does not purport to be an historical account of my years at P.M.C. but is above all, a work of imagination.

INTRODUCTION TO THE SECOND EDITION

Since the publication of *Rooks*, I've had the opportunity to examine the special P.M.C. archives, located at Widener University. I've also exchanged e-mails, letters, and phone calls with former cadets who read *Rooks* and shared anecdotes, opinions, and minutiae with me. These exchanges, along with the primary source materials in the archives, provided me with ideas for new poems, and fresh motivation to publish a revised and expanded 2nd Edition.

This book is dedicated to my dear friend and fellow member of the Class of 1967, Ronald "Ray" Petrauskas (1945-1990).

I stand on a hill, watch and keep still,
And the sun laughs, having covered everything
With blood, and cannons roll down the road,
And battalions sing, and guns glitter.

from *War Years*, by Henrikas Radauskas,
translated from the Lithuanian
by Jonas Zdanys

PART 1

Pennsylvania Military College

Pennsylvania Military College Stadium

Color Cadet Guard & Howell Hall Dormitory
Pennsylvania Military College
Chester, PA

THE PROMOTIONAL PAMPHLET

Photo *of a teacher with his arm*
around a student, blackboard
covered with algebraic formulas.

Cadets having their rifles inspected.
"acute mind, many-sided education,
each course taught by a full-fledged professor."

Photo *of a football player*
crashing through a line of tacklers,
bleachers filled with cheering cadets.

"the whole man, camaraderie of belonging,
develop self-discipline, personal poise,
sense of self-confidence."

Photo *of an Army officer,*
chest radiant with ribbons,
swagger stick held behind his back.

"guidance, but no coddling,
leadership, but no hazing,
pride of the uniform, spirit and character."

"within close proximity of Philadelphia,
PMC: the West Point of the Keystone State."

R O O K S

LAST FAMILY VACATION, 1963

I sink into a cow pie
on an Amish farm,
have a sneezing fit
on the battlefields of Gettysburg,
sicken myself on chocolate
at Hershey Park.

The last place I want to be
is away from my friends
and the drag strips of Connecticut
in an unair-conditioned Ford
with my father, mother and sister.

Things pick up at the Eagle Theater
in Philly, where I hear Bobby Rydell
sing "Kissin' Time,"and "Wild One,"
and ogle the girls in the aisles
dancing the Bristol Stomp.

On our way home, my father stops
at Pennsylvania Military College,
where in less than two months
I'll start as a fledgling cadet.

Two officers show us around,
"friendly chaps" — my dad says,
talk about the code of the gentleman:
duty, honor, leadership,
one of them winks,
"Girls can't resist a uniform."

At the parade grounds
I watch the Pershing Rifles practice,
national drill team champions,
every step in quick time,
dust puffs rising from their heels,
like dirt turned up by a machine gun.

ROOKS

FIRST MONTH

I'm slumped at my desk
on the Third Floor of Howell Hall
puffing Lucky Strikes
one after the other.
I stare out the window
listening to children's laughter
and the thump of a basketball
coming from a playground
across the railroad tracks.

I'm brooding about
the guys at home,
the girlfriend I lost,
my mom's good cooking,
the '55 Chevy I outfitted
with a 425 horsepower engine
I sold dirt cheap
the day before starting my rook year.

My face festers with pimples,
bloody nicks dot my chin
my hair is cut back to the bone
— white walls, they call them.
I tick off the Lucky Strikes:
…eighteen, nineteen…

Last on my list of college picks,
I chose Pennsylvania Military College
because the catalogue said
it had a weightlifting team
and I'm an iron pumper.
But when I arrive
the team has been phased out.

My father set the trap
talking up his five-year stint
in the cavalry
clip-clopping through America.
Discipline would force me
to be a better student, I thought,
grow a set of balls,
be a leader.

A train shuffles by.
I crumple the letter I just received
from Paulette's new boyfriend
informing me that since they are engaged
it's not right that I keep writing her.
I'm about to light up another Lucky
when the door explodes
and in strides Sergeant Kotowski.

"Ten-shun!" my roommate shouts.
We spring up.
"Eyes straight ahead!
What are you looking at?
You a Mary, or somethin'?
Chin in, suck in that gut,
pinch those shoulders,
I want to see sweat!"

The train shrieks.
 "What did I tell you 'bout looking straight ahead?
Now drop for twenty!"
I hit the floor
my arms shaking
pumping up/down.
The Sarge bends over me
ticks off,
"...two, three, four..."

PROFILE

I couldn't stop nodding
that first day in uniform
at McMorland Student Center,
hearing you go on
about honor, duty, flag,
a staff sergeant shook me awake so hard
I thought my neck would snap.

Commandant, two-star general
at the reviewing stand,
steel-straight nose,
your slight stoop of imperial boredom,
the swagger stick gripped like a scepter.

Your silhouette,
a backdrop to marching music,
dress parades, present arms,
hallucinations of draft notices,
napalm, the drizzle of Agent Orange,
your voice droning on.

SPIT SHINES

I twist off the shoe polish cap
where I've embedded
a penny in black wax
following a century-old tradition
that claims a copper coin
keeps the oil from drying up.

On Oxford shoes, I apply
a foundation coat of wax
then wrap my index finger
in a cotton handkerchief
skim off a pat of polish
and with circular motions
blend water and wax into leather
until the glaze resembles polished onyx.

To preserve their shape,
I place wooden shoe trees
inside the spit-shined Oxfords.
To keep off the dust, I drape a face cloth
over the luminous leather.
After reveille I unveil the spit shines,
hold them up to my mouth
breathe on the toe tips
and with a soft rag
give them a good buffing.

At morning muster, Sergeant Kotowski
swaggers up to me
points to a speck of dust on one shoe
"Hey, douche bag,
what did you polish your shoes with,
Brillo pads?"

SQUARE MEALS

Military discipline
gives me indigestion
and the Mess Head at my table
denounces my defiant looks
ordering me to eat a square meal.

I sit erect my eyes straight ahead
and with an outstretched arm
bring my shit-on-a-shingle
— chipped beef on toast —
straight up and straight in
with a mechanical box-like motion.

It's hit or miss, soon my shirt
with three creases according
to military mandate
is spattered with globs
of what looks like sea gull droppings.

I grimace after a piece of beef
wedges under my collar
and the Mess Head
in a fury of "Raunchy-ass
rook mammy-jammer!"
orders me to eat under the table.

I sit in the shadows among
the mirror glows of spit shine shoes
my arm above the table
fork moving up and down
heavy with the sound
of upperclassmen's laughter.

GIL FAGIANI

WHITE GLOVE INSPECTION

All Friday night we prepare
for Saturday's white glove inspection:
We wash and wax the floor,
sponge out the strip of linoleum
under the radiator,
clean every crevice, crack and page
of our desks, shelves and books,
tighten our bed spreads
till a quarter bounces off them,
fold our underclothes into rectangles
one inch high, four inches wide,
swab the ceiling and walls with a moist mop.

When the door opens
Captain Doyle and his entourage enter,
we stand throbbing with pride: brass bright
shoes like burnished marble,
gray uniforms crisscrossed with white belts.

Captain Doyle stands without moving
his eyes rake the four corners of our room.
"Screwdriver!"
The words are barely out of his mouth
before Corporal Heller hands him
a green plastic-handled screwdriver.

Picking up our radio,
he unscrews the back cover
inserts his gloved finger deep into its interior
and withdraws his finger
displaying a grayish smudge.
"Ten demerits, and weekend restriction."
Then pivots on his heels and leaves.

[continued]

ROOKS

Later that night I lay on my bunk
watching dust particles
twinkle around the bare bulb
of the ceiling light.

WEAK LINK

"OK, dirtbags,"
Sergeant Kotowski shrieks,
"somebody left a pubic hair on the toilet seat
Everyone out of bed!
and against the hallway wall!"

"You wanna be little piggies?"
Eyes forward!
Tuck in your chins!
Arms straight by your sides!
Pinch those shoulders back!
Suck in your guts!"

Lids flicker,
faces redden,
veins bulge,
limbs quiver,
sweat trickles.

After thirty minutes
chicken-chested
chain-smoking Alexander Orlov
gasps, loosens up, lets out his chin.
"O.K., mister, hit the floor!
Give me ten push-ups!"

Orlov gets on the floor
raises up on his broomstick arms
does three push-ups,
collapses.

[continued]

ROOKS

"The rest of you rooks
give me twenty push-ups!"
All the freshmen clamber
on the floor grunting
and bunting the linoleum
until they pump out
twenty pushups.

"What's the matter, your pussies hurt?
Nobody gets up until Orlov
knocks off his ten pushups!"
Another thirty minutes go by
before the freshmen,
their arms as limp
as damp bath towels,
return to their rooms.

Orlov climbs into his bunk
head heavy
with curses, and threats
to bust his faggot-ass.

GIL FAGIANI

SOUL MUSIC

Holed up in my barrack's bunker,
I tune my radio to WDAS
one of Philly's three soul stations
my military bearing melting to the heat
of Sam and Dave's "I'm Coming,"
Jackie Wilson's "Baby Work Out."

Too uptight to use the hallway latrine,
I fear running into an upperclassman
who on a lark might ask me
to stare at a wall crack for an hour,
kiss the floor for a dozen push-ups,
sound off by memory military regs.

Any stray facial motion, yawn, tic, or spasm,
can be interpreted as quibbling, attitude, disobedience
resulting in a deluge of demerit slips
followed by punishment tours —
hour-long marches in parking lots,
work details, weekend restrictions.

So I urinate in a coffee can
hide out in my room snapping my fingers
to Shirley Ellis' "The Real Nitty Gritty,"
Ko Ko Taylor's "Wing Dang Doodle."

One evening I empty my can out the window
and a series of violent knocks
convulses the third corridor of Howell Hall.

I lower the volume to the Wicked Pickett's
"I'm a Midnight Mover,"
as Lieutenant Colonel Michael Hunter
goes from door to door
his service cap and jacket
shiny with wet patches.

3 1

ROOKS

INTELLECTUAL COMBAT

"College is the market-
place of ideas, the clash
of opposing viewpoints,"
the President says in his address
to the freshman class.
My Military Science prof. says,
"The United States Army
never lost a war."
"What about Korea?" I ask.
"You're out of order," he says.
"Wasn't it a stalemate?"
"One more word out of you
and your ass is out the door."

GIL FAGIANI

THE DAY JFK WAS SHOT

The Major makes us laugh,
saying a strategic withdrawal
is what the Army calls retreat,
though, he adds, as cadets
the concept of defeat is off limits.

The walls of our Quonset hut classroom
are too thin to keep out
the November wind
and when Military Theory is over
I hurry off to the barracks.

On a pathway I meet Jeb,
his eyes dark and glary as his spit shines,
who tells me the President was hit
by a gunman put up by Castro and the Russkies.

Before I can respond, he says
he bumped into a Spanish student
— probably Cuban —
who smiled when told JFK was shot,
and seizing the element of surprise,
punched the commie cockroach
down a flight of stairs.

ROOKS

BARRACKS' SCRIBE

Fever flows in my fingers.
For months I dash off
flowery letters,
first to my girl,
your unsurpassable pulchritude,
then to my ex-girl,
the imperishable flame of love
then at my buddies' requests,
to their girls,
golden ringlets and radiant visage.

But my buddies' girls
break off with them,
one by one, dumping us all
in the same pot
of pain and loneliness.
To lighten the mood
I pen pretend suicide notes,
ending eighteen years
of petty schemes
and puerile frustrations.

GIL FAGIANI

THANKSGIVING FURLOUGH

First time home since I enter P.M.C:
Mess Hall grease oozes out of my skin
creating a mountain chain of zits,
my hair is sheared down to my skull
like I had psycho-surgery.

Nobody's in the neighborhood.
My best buddy's already at war,
shot in the hand at the Bay of Saigon
while painting the side of his boat.
I'm so tired from pre-dawn drills
and midnight push-up parties
that I sleep twelve hours a day.
My aunts resent me when I refuse
to be photographed in uniform.

I visit my ex-girlfriend in Danbury
who sings a duet with her fiancée
while he plays the piano
in front of her father and mother
who toast the smiling couple
with glasses of peppermint schnapps
while I hide in a cloud of cigarette smoke.

At night I go to a bar in Brewster
chasing shots of Henessey with ale
until carried out the side door
like a sack of empty beer bottles.
I heave myself through hedges
trip over tree roots
pass out on Route 51
my legs straight and my arms out
roused by two cops
kicking me into consciousness.

ROOKS

MURRAY THE K'S HOLIDAY REVUE

We hurtle towards Brooklyn
in Joe-Joe's Volkswagen Bug
guzzling cans of Rheingiold
braying donkeys of happiness
without our upperclass tormentors.

Below the marquee
of the Brooklyn Fox Theater
police on horseback fight to keep surging fans
from flooding Flatbush Avenue.

Yolk-yellow bulbs bathe the names in light:
Smokey Robinson and the Miracles, the Marvelettes,
Screaming Jay Hawkins, Chuck Jackson,
Dionne Warwick, Mary Wells, the Shangri-Las.

When wooden barricades fall we join
the stampede through brass doors,
charging down aisles smelling of Dixie Peach,
Acquanet, Wildroot Cream Oil.

A holdout from an earlier show
refuses to budge from her front row seat.
We watch as a uniformed guard pulls on her arm,
leveraging his big butt to raise her skinny one,
never expecting the uppercut to his jaw.

Later Murray shimmies into the lights
with his arms around Dionne,
her cheekbones high, hair swept back, pants tight.
Joe-Joe jumps up, "She's the Devil!"

Spotlights crisscross the stage.
Chuck throws first his tie,
then his jacket to his fans,
the crowd roars, "Do the Monkey!" to the Miracles'
choreographed mugging,
and Screaming Jay shrieks, "I'm Gonna Put a Spell on You!"

BLAME

Sunday afternoon.
Sacked out in my bunk.
Peaceful,
no drills, inspections,
heckling, ridicule.

Tapping on my door.
I open an eye.
It's not an upperclassman
they'd storm in without knocking.
I bury my face in the pillow.
The tapping grows louder.
Jump up.
"Who the fuck is it?"

Door opens.
A man in rimless glasses
steps in, jaw tight as a slingshot.
It's my roommate's father.
"I'm sorry, sir, I thought…"
"Do you know where Skip is?"
"No, sir, I…"
He makes an about-face.

I'm summoned to the Commandant.
He tells me my roommate quit the corps,
his father complains:
I turned our room into a hangout,
played the radio too loud,
kept his son from studying,
used vile language.

GIL FAGIANI

NIGHT OF THE HOT HOAGIE

Every night, chest out, face shiny,
Brigade Sergeant Samuel L. Silverman
bursts into my room
10 p.m. hunger hour
while I stand eyes forward,
gut in, shoulders back,
quivering like I have palsy.
Sergeant Silverman sniffs around
for a Philly-style hoagie sandwich:
cheese steak, shrimp salad,
hamburger, Italian.

He opens drawers
looks in coat pockets
lifts up blankets and sheets
when he finds a hoagie
confiscates half declaring: "R.H.I.P"
— Rank Has Its Privileges —
as the big knot in his throat
works itself up and down
and half my precious sandwich
disappears down his gullet.

Fed up with being ripped off,
I order an Italian flame-thrower
from Fran and Nan's Hoagie Shop:
prosciutto, salami, and provolone
all three layers larded with Tabasco,
Louisiana Hot Sauce,
and cherry peppers.

[continued]

ROOKS

The next evening Sergeant Silverman
bursts into my room
picking up the scent of hoagie.
I make no attempt to hide it.
After the first few bites Sarge roars
and runs off to the latrine
where he latches his lips around
the cold water faucet.

PART 2

The cadet corps forms a guard of honor in front of Old Main just before the Academic Procession starts.

PMC Cadets Marching c. 1917

The cadets and graduates drill on the parade ground before a reviewing body of faculty and alumni of the college, while friends in the grandstand watch.

Retiring Bishop Francis M. Taitt, who participated in the College Commencement exercises, Donald Nelson of the U. S. War Production Board who received an honorary Doctor of Laws degree, and Joseph Grundy Shryock, president of Belmont Iron Works who received an honorary Doctor of Science in Engineering, watch the drilling of the cadet corps.

GIL FAGIANI

SPOONING ON THE SMELLY JELLY

I room with a cadet named Blair
known to everyone as Bear
because every inch of him is covered with hair
even his knees and elbows.

Raised on a dairy farm
Bear speaks with a heavy drawl
tells me a tale about necking
with his girl backwoods style.

It's a moonlit night.
Bear borrows his pa's pickup
and with his arm around his new girl
drives to the edge of a woods
overlooking a clover field.
They start to neck — spooning — they call it.
Bear decides to sit with her
on the straw-covered bed of the pickup
in case things get serious.

As they slap and tickle
Bear leans backward with his girl
feels something soft and sticky
on his shoulders. The air turns rank.
"It was some pretty smelly jelly," Bear says.
"I helped pa that morning
deliver a calf in the barn
shoveling the cow's afterbirth
into the pickup's bed."

Afterwards I could never look at Bear
stretched out on his bunk again
without wrinkling my nose.

R O O K S

SUCKER PUNCH

The tallest rooks in Alfa Company
Jeb and Ted stand side by side
in the rear squad of their platoon.

Jeb is gung ho and joins the Rangers.
In high school he studied judo,
no cadet can hold out
against his reverse hip throw
or parry his thrusts in bayonet drill.

Son of "Displaced Persons,"
Ted's parents fled Lithuania
after the Nazis showed up.
He grew up in a seedy section
of Elizabeth, New Jersey, with other D.P. brats
fought turf wars with Ukies, Pollocks
Wops, Shines, and Ricans.

Jeb holds Ted in disdain
for coming to morning formations
with scummy brass, scuffed shoes
a stubbly face
that looks like he shaves with a sea shell.

When the Commandant calls Bravo Company
the embodiment of the Corps' finest traditions.
Jeb blabs to platoon mates
that Ted has run down Alfa's competitive edge.
Ted blabs back that Jeb is a military robot.

Clenching his fists,
Jeb calls Ted out
they set a date
to steal away to the stadium
to go to war on the parade grounds.

Jeb shows up in Ranger gear:
fatigues
blue beret
camouflage ascot
spit-shined combat boots.
Ted wears his standard issue cap and gray jacket.

They run down a ramp toward the grassy field
as Ted throws a punch to the right side of Jeb's face.
Staggered, Jeb repositions himself
unleashes a roundhouse that misses its mark
and smashes into an iron railing.·

For next morning's formation
Jeb's right arm is in a cast
from his shoulder to his finger tips.
He tells everyone who will listen
that he broke his hand on Ted's head.
Ted remains mum
but when they march into the Mess Hall
he steps on Jeb's spit shines.

SMOKERS

Our reg book places great emphasis
on maintaining the highest moral values.
Coarse language is frowned upon.
Porn mags are forbidden.
Church squad is mandatory.

So I was surprised
when Corporal Heller
announced that freshmen
who pay a dollar are welcome
to enter the lieutenant's room
and watch a smoker.

We sit in t-shirts
on the polished linoleum floor
— buffed with freshmen elbow grease —
awkward with the strange
lapse in military formality.

A small projector throws
grainy pictures on the wall.
The first title is, "Pole Vaulting"
a naked man with a foot-long phallus
lays on the floor while
a long succession of women
impale themselves on him.

The second is, "Tongue Bath,"
a naked man with a foot-long phallus
stands up and a bevy of babes
kneel before him licking his crotch
like cattle lapping a salt lick.

GIL FAGIANI

The third, "Ice cream Sandwich"
a white woman gets down
on her hands and knees
while two naked black men
with foot-long phalluses
enter her from the back and front.

Except for the steady creaking
of the projector's reels
the room falls silent
until the film ends
and the freshmen rise
filing out the door in unison.

ROOKS

STANDARDS

Military college exchange week.
Banners of a half dozen schools
wave in front of Old Main.
A cadet officer from South Carolina
bunks with me for three days.
He prides himself with preserving
the highest standard of military appearance
as befits what he boasts is the best
military institution of higher learning in the U.S:
The Citadel.

His cap visor blazing with Bryl-Cream.
His head and face hairless as a honeydew.
His uniform with carving-knife creases.
His brass pips dazzling like gold ducats.
His shoes punched out of mirror-polished molds.

To master the problem
of free-falling dust mites
blighting the black braid
running down his trouser legs,
thirty or forty time a day
he tears off a piece of tape
from the Scotch Tape dispenser
never far from his lacquered finger nails
and rubs it along the side of his pants.

GIL FAGIANI

THE SALUTE

I drink to the uniform
to the drabness of life
to the mangling of my name
at every roll call,
and to you, Captain Doyle
I raise a glass —
you swore you'd drive me out of the corps.
You made me march double-time
rifle over my head,
stand at attention for hours,
do hundreds of push-ups,
and when I wouldn't break,
ordered me to squat in your room
arms out, palms up
holding a wooden shelf
loaded with Army manuals,
your eyes burning
— I never dropped a book.

ROOKS

LOCAL GIRLS

They are the daughters of Ukrainian,
Lithuanian and Polish parents
who pull double shifts
in front of the blast furnaces
of Penn State Casting,
the rolling mills of Scott Paper,
the monster cranes of Sun Ship,
the cable spools of Reynolds Metals.

Teased beehive hairdos
and bubblegum perfume,
they speed back and forth in front
of cadet barracks in banged-up Chevies
and Fords their eyes avoiding
the eyes of cadets who call them
Chester Whore Rats
from both sides of Fourteenth Street.

Driving by, they hunker down
below the dashboard
to avoid the slobber of cadet wolf whistles
and plow into the back of another car
braking for a stop sign
at the corner of Melrose.

The gnashing steel and shattering glass
signals the cadets to surround
the two car-loads of girls
hollering their heads off
till the Assistant Commandant
double-times it to the intersection
and waves away their assailants
like dispersing a cloud of locusts.

GIL FAGIANI

THE ASTERISK

Prodigious weightlifter
I place in the top tenth
of my class in military exercises
peerless
in the hand grenade throw
running the obstacle course
repelling with a rope off the stadium wall.

When a flu rages through the barracks
laying low most of my classmates
I'm the last to hold out
but feverish and flat on my back
I end up in the infirmary.

After three days my class advisor
Army Captain James D. Connolly calls:
"Cadet #222,
reviewing my roll book
I see a big asterisk
in front of your name
I'm calling to confirm your status:"

"Sick, sir."
"Carry on, then."

ROOKS

A TANK COMES
TO PENNSYLVANIA MILITARY COLLEGE

Ordered as a teaching tool,
the thirty-five ton, M 4,
medium vehicle of the Sherman class,
chugs down the ramp of the flatbed truck
onto the parking lot behind Howell Hall.

The tank tears up asphalt
stops on a grassy knoll,
its 76 millimeter cannon
and three machine guns
overlooking the railway tracks,
the deserted schoolyard,
the decaying row houses,
of downtown Chester.

With a final shudder,
the engine cuts off
a black cloud of smoke
hangs in the air.
I kneel and pull out
a handful of golden-yellow
daisy faces, crushed
in the imprints of tank treads.

GIL FAGIANI

UKRAINIAN HALL

Since the penalty for drinking is immediate dismissal,
Ted and I hang out at the Chester Arms, a rundown hotel
filled with prostitutes, petty hustlers and transvestites in
the black part of town, where the booze is cheap, the
jukebox cooking, and the chances of seeing a proper
cadet officer about as likely as an on-campus draft-card
burning. Ted is away that weekend, and I decide to go
alone to a local dance at the Ukrainian Hall in spite of
Ted's warnings about "the Ukies," which, because he is
Lithuanian, I shrug off as the paranoid product of some
exotic Eastern European rivalry. Soon after I arrive at the
vast Hall, a line of drunken louts with beer pitchers in
their hands push toward a single wooden cask that with-
in minutes goes dry setting off a melee of cries, curses,
and flying chairs. Fights break out everywhere, and after
somebody smashes a glass pitcher over the guy's head
next to me and waves the bloody handle at me. I leap
out a side window and run past the stretch of two-story
frame houses, the outer border of the white section of
town.

"WON'T BE LONG NOW!"

Short and skeletal,
with a muddy complexion
a mouth twisted
into a permanent grin,
Eddie walks with a limp
that makes his left shoulder dip.

A groundskeeper
for as long as anyone can remember,
he could usually be found
pushing a garbage cart
in the parking lot behind the stadium.

As much a fixture
on the P.M.C. campus
as the mortar
the howitzer
the tank
the Victorian monstrosity
known as Old Main.

Eddie comes from Chester's
black community
compared by some
to South Africa's Soweto Township
with its heaps of litter and rot
in front of ghetto houses.
There are no black members
of Chester's fire department
during "civil rights disturbances"
the police call their batons
"nigger sticks."

I first met Eddie
a few days before Christmas Furlough
on my way back from classes.
"Won't be long now!" he says.
"That's right," I reply, "Can't wait
to get away from this dump."

Ten days later I return from furlough
run into Eddie
in the shadows of the Stadium wall
standing by his garbage cart,
bristling with dead branches.

 "Won't be long now!"
I give him a weak smile
look away
continue back to my barracks.

A week later,
I cut across the stadium's parking lot
see Eddie by his cart.
"Won't be long now!"
And something about his rickety cart
his dipping left shoulder
his frozen grin
makes me think of smoke-filled streets
police sirens
flying bricks
bloody white faces.

SPRING PARADE

Gray-clad arms and legs
move in perfect coordination
to the cocky beat of a phalanx
of white-belted drummers.
Cadet photographer Edwin Pitts
shadows our ranks
as we march off campus
in our Dress A uniforms
our brass buttons gleaming
our hat plumes swaying
in the flower-scented spring breeze.

We wind through the dirty streets
of downtown Chester
a boomtown during the war years
now sliding toward depression
as shipyards and steel mills
close down one after another.

On the sidewalks,
a few passersby move
to the beat of the drummers.
Some kids laugh,
do a defiant dance in the street.
At City Hall we halt
while the shutterbug snaps a picture
of the Commandant switching
his swagger stick
from his right to left
and shaking hands with the mayor.

Drums rumble.
We march off again
strutting through empty back streets.
Cadet photographer Pitts
his back to a railroad tunnel
clicks off panoramic shots
of the cadet corps
but is unable to gauge the distance
of the oncoming train
because of the tunnel's echo.
Before he can jump out of the way
he is struck by the hurtling diesel.

Back on campus
word seeps through the ranks
of the death of our classmate.
Our morale wilts
along with the drum beat
that now sounds a funeral dirge
as we march into the Mess Hall
with no appetite for our gala meal
of grisly steak and melting ice cream.

ROOKS

VIETNAM

A lone protester
at 14th and Chestnut
carries a sign
"Stop the Bombing!"

Cadets return from class
go on the attack
leave protester's long hair
plastered to gashed forehead
groping for his glasses
among roots of an oak tree
wet with dog piss.

As chipped beef coagulates
in front of my eyes
I hear Mess Hall buzz,
pals boast: mobile defense,
pincer movement,
war of annihilation,
while the Major orders us
to cease and desist
military action against peacenik
since "what scum like this
want most of all
is publicity for their filthy cause."

GIL FAGIANI

THE CHESTER ARMS

A hot spring night at the Chester Arms.
Somebody jacks up the volume of the jukebox
and the room rocks to the sounds
of the Isley Brothers preaching
the gospel of pussy,
Chuck Jackson's "Beg Me."
I unbutton the collar of my uniform.

Joyce, slim, dark and doe-eyed sits across from me,
I can't keep my legs still.
She argues with one of her johns,
an Italian construction worker
covered with dirt and curly black hair.

The john pulls on her arm
spilling her Cutty Sark and milk
she bounces a shot glass off his chest.
Mike, the bartender, takes his baseball bat
comes from behind the counter
and pushes them both out the door.

Avoiding the stares
of two brawny transvestites,
I listen to Perry, a regular, boast
about his college days
when he drove a Porsche
and styled himself the Prince of Poon Tang.

[continued]

ROOKS

I feed the juke box quarters
and down balls and beers
Perry insists on paying for.
Out of the corner of my eye
I watch his wife,
a grizzly bear in a blonde wig,
hitting on every stud at the bar
wondering when Perry is going to snap
and go upside her head.

Leaving to piss,
I return to Otis Redding's
"...gotta, gotta have it..."
the bass so loud the bar glasses rumble.
I hear scuffling in the lobby
and through a Dutch door
see Perry whale away
on one of the men his wife flirted with.

Buttoning my collar, I'm ready to split
when Perry's wife backs me against the wall
shoves her hand between my legs,
"I hear cadet cock's the best there is,"
her wig as crooked as her smile.

GIL FAGIANI

RIFFING ON THE RULE BOOK

Memorandums
detail lists, demerit lists
exercise of command
interior guard orders
general orders, special orders
punishment orders, orders of the day

Military courtesy
acts of high moral courage
delinquencies, disrespect for colors
boards of investigation
Commandant's boards, brigade boards
quibbling

Sick call, sick in quarters
mess formations
parade formations, drill formations
cadet promotions, cadet reductions
staff sergeants, platoon leaders, color corporals
Saturday inspections
uniform inspections
daily room inspections

Absent duty, neglect of duty
Dress A, Dress White
red sash, sword and scabbard
chevrons and class stripes
garrison cap
badges, medals, service ribbons
academic star, aviation wing, ranger patch

ROOKS

RANK

Rumors ripple
through the long gray line
that a few days before I return
as a newly-minted corporal,
a freshman
unable to take the orientation,
the training,
stood on a chair
in Howell Hall
with an electrical cord around his neck
and hanged himself.

There was no official mention of his death
no announcement at assembly
or Mess Hall
nothing on the radio, TV
or newspapers.

It was as though
he were a summer fly
who one day
when the weather changed
fell to the bottom of the windowsill.

GIL FAGIANI

SPRING OFFENSIVE, 1967

Mess III.
Rainbow of grease.
Gangrene-colored spinach.
Chicken for the fifth time in a week.
Ted grabs his gut,
"I can't eat this shit."

He tosses a napkin.
Somebody else, a slice of bread.
I stand up, "Bomb the brass!"
pitch softball-sized potatoes
at the elevated tables in front
where the honchos sit,
the spuds splat against the wall
the Colonel's face calcifying.

The air fills with plates, cups, glasses,
knives ricochet across the floor.
Troops vomiting curses,
their tongues like battle flags,
their arms blurry from throwing.
A cadet officer stumbles on the mic
"When finished rioting, the corps is dismissed."
Then the lights go out.

At the Chester Diner,
over bottles of Budweiser
and fried salami slices,
Ted points to the TV:
smoldering hamlets, firefights,
arms dangling from gurneys,
body counts, body counts, body counts.

MUSIC SOURCES

"Kissin' Time," Bobby Rydell.
"Wild One," Bobby Rydell.
"Bristol Stomp," Dovells.
"I'm Coming," Sam and Dave.
"Baby Work Out," Jackie Wilson.
"The Real Nitty-Gritty," Shirley Ellis.
"Wing Dang Doodle," Ko Ko Taylor.
"I'm a Midnight Mover," Wilson Pickett.
"Don't Make Me Over," Dion Warwick.
"Mickey's Monkey," Smokey Robinson and the Miracles.
"I'm Gonna Put a Spell on You," Screaming Jay Hawkins.
"Too Many Fish in the Sea," Marvelettes.
"You Beat Me to the Punch," Mary Wells.
"Leader of the Pack," Shangri-Las.
"Beg Me," Chuck Jackson.
"Twistin' With Linda," Isley Brothers.
"I Can't Turn You Loose," Otis Redding.

APPENDIX:
ALUMNI DEATHS
IN VIETNAM

Capt. Daniel F. Monahan '62 Killed By Land Mine in Action in Vietnam

Once again, the tragic toll of the war in Vietnam has struck home at PMC in all its terrifying intensity with news of the death of Capt. Daniel F. Monahan '62.

A career officer, and member of the elite Special Forces "Green Berets," he was killed by a land mine in Vietnam on April 14. Heightening the tragedy is the fact that his wife, Elizabeth, had given birth to a girl only eight days before.

At Pennsylvania Military College, Dan was a Business Administration major, a Distinguished Military student, and was voted the outstanding cadet of the senior class at ROTC encampment. He was a member of the Glee Club, Chess Club and S.A.M., played intramural football for four years, and was a member of the track team during his freshman year.

Immediately following graduation, in June 1962, he joined the Army and received a regular U. S. Army commission of 2/Lt.

He was transferred to Vietnam, shortly after he and his wife returned to his parents' home in Glenolden, Pa., from an 18-month tour of duty in Panama. He had been in Vietnam for four months.

Besides his wife, daughter Maureen, and his parents, Francis and Edith Monahan, he is survived by a sister, Mrs. Eleanor Cantarella, of Haddon Heights, N. J.

Funeral services on April 24 were attended by an honor guard from PMC.

CAPT. DANIEL F. MONAHAN '62

GIL FAGIANI

OBITUARIES

1917 — Dr. Frank Wilcoxon
— Mrs. Robert T. Tumbelston
1963 — Lt. William J. Stephenson

WILLIAM J. (Buddy) STEPHENSON

The terrible cost of the war in Viet Nam has been brought home again to the hearts of the men of PMC.

Buddy Stephenson has paid the supreme sacrifice and leaves all who knew and loved him grieved, but proud that he died in the service of his country.

A member of the Class of '63 (which also lost its brigade commander, John L. Geoghegan, on the Viet Nam battle field), Buddy Stephenson is well remembered on campus for his vitality, his skill with the trumpet (he played for the marching band and the dance band), his industry and honesty. An accounting major, he was also in the Glee Club and was a member of the football, wrestling and track teams.

He leaves behind his wife, Carol, and a two-year-old son.

2/LT. JOHN L. GEOGHEGAN '63
Viet Nam Casualty

The sad news of the death of John Lance Geoghegan has brought the meaning of the war in Viet Nam to the heart of P.M.C. Jack fell on 15 November, 1965, during the bitter fighting in the central highlands near Chu Pong Mountain. He was serving as a Platoon Leader in Co. "C," 1st Bn., 7th Cavalry (Air Mobile). Many will remember him as the Brigade Commander in 1963, when General Eisenhower visited the campus. The entire PMC family, faculty, students and alumni are saddened by the loss of a young man so full of promise.

John Geoghegan died for his country; no greater honor can come to any man.

GIL FAGIANI

Lieut. David R. Wilson '66 Killed By Mortar Fire in Central Vietnam

1/Lt. David R. Wilson '66 lost his life in the Vietcong offensive in Central Vietnam on Jan. 31. He died as the result of multiple fragmentation wounds received when a vehicle in which he was riding came under heavy mortar attack between An Khe and Pleiku.

Funeral services were held on Feb. 20 in Christ Lutheran Church, Oreland, Pa.

Members of the colleges' administration, faculty and staff, and the Commandant's staff, attended the services. Six Cadets who served as pall bearers were: Charles Cantley, Thomas Dougherty, James Mady, John Parry, John Pierson and William Potts.

Cadets William Feyk and Stuart Perlmutter were buglers.

Lieut. Wilson is survived by his parents, Mr. and Mrs. David M. Wilson, Jr., 311 Lorraine Avenue, Oreland, and a sister who is the wife of Joseph C. Holler '64.

In lieu of flowers at the funeral, his parents requested that donations be sent to Christ Lutheran Church or Pennsylvania Military College.

As a student, Lieut. Wilson was Cadet Aide to Commandant Menard. A member of Tau Kappa Epsilon, he was treasurer of the Theta Lambda Chapter in his junior and senior years. He also was a member of the Circle K Club and the Society for Advancement of Management.

Lieut. Wilson is the fifth alumnus to lose his life in the Vietnam conflict. Others are: Lt. (j.g.) Joseph R. Mossman '61, Lt. John L. Geoghegan '63, Lt. William J. Stephenson '63 and Capt. Daniel F. Monahan '62.

Gil Fagiani attended Pennsylvania Military College from 1963 to 1967. He is a poet, short story writer, essayist and translator. His poetry has appeared in such anthologies as *Off the Cuffs: Poetry by and about the Police*, edited by Jackie Sheeler, and *Sweet Lemons: Writings With a Sicilian Accent*, edited by Venera Fazio and Delia De Santis.

In 2004 a collection of his poetry set in East Harlem in the 1960's: *Crossing 116th Street: A Blanquito in El Barrio*, was published in the literary journal *Skidrow Penthouse*. In 2005, he won an "Honorable Mention" for both the Allen Ginsberg Poetry Awards, and the Bordighera Prize.

Fagiani co-hosts the monthly open reading of the Italian American Writers' Association at the Cornelia Street Café, in New York City, and is the associate editor of the literary arts journal *Feile-Festa*. His translations of nine poems from Abruzzese dialect to English were published last year in *The Journal of Italian Translation* edited by Luigi Bonaffini.

A social worker by profession, Gil directs a treatment program for recovering drug addicts and alcoholics in downtown Brooklyn.

Readers are encouraged to share their reactions to "ROOKS" with the author at rookspmc@aol.com

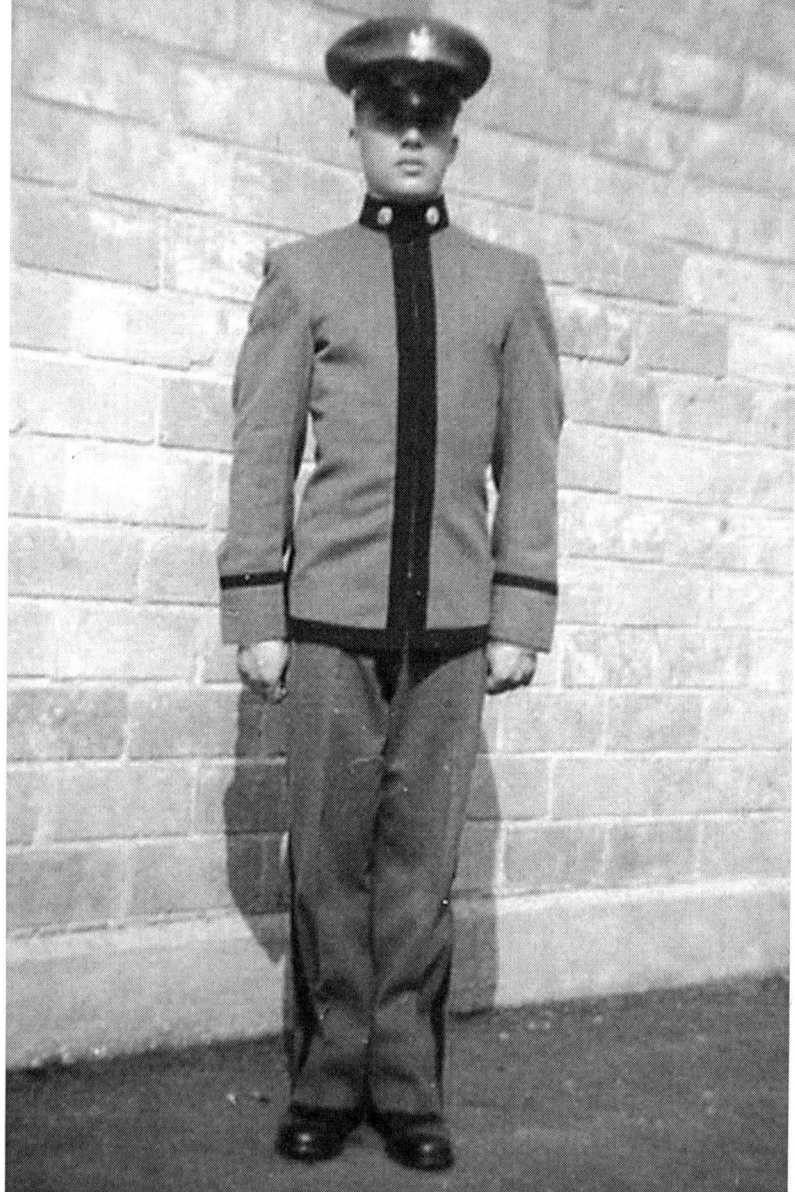